Stay Sane Through Change®

for

LEADERS

How to use periods of change to steer your organization into a rock solid position

Tolu Adeleye, Ph.D.

Also by Tolu Adeleye, Ph.D.

Stay Sane Through Change: How to Rise Above the Challenges of Life's Complex Transitions

Strength to Deliver: How to Revive and Give Birth to Your Interrupted Dreams

Career Transition Gems: Insider Secrets to a Successful Career Change

Sanity and Strength: Wisdom to Get Unstuck and Power to Move on from the Muddy Paths of Life Transitions

Stay Sane Through Change® Series

Table of Contents

Chapter One

Introduction

When I first co-authored the first <u>Stay Sane Through Change</u> book (1), my co-author and I had the mission of using it to help individuals use times of change as stepping stones to a greater fulfillment in life. While many more *Stay Sane Through Change* ® products have become available since the launch of that first product, the mission of the brand remains the same. Over the course of more than ten years, many individuals have been blessed by the empowering message that was an output of the mission. Not only has this brand blessed others, but I as the purveyor of the brand and equipper of others have been blessed on a personal level as well. Indeed I have been able to rise above the many challenges of a number of complex transitions that have come my way.

What I have identified over the past years of working and promoting *Stay Sane Through Change* ® products is the dare need to inculcate the principles of staying `sane through *change* in people who have leadership roles. I have found it essential to equip these leaders of all dimensions with tools that will enable them to excel when handling both *internal* and *external* changes. This nudge and fresh awakening have come as a result of a number of circumstantial events. Firstly, on a personal note, I have re-discovered many golden nuggets for rising above the challenges of change in my personal and career leadership engagements. Secondly, while working with a number of emerging leaders, I have been able to help them use some key principles to stay sane through different periods of change that they were going through in their personal and professional lives.

In more recent times, I have come to recognize in a myriad of ways that all these personal and professional experiences are 'not about me' at all. In fact, at some point in one of the recent challenges I faced, I was literally 'shipwrecked and catapulted onto a lonely island'. Once I managed to elope from that island, I hit the ground running and was ready to launch forth into a fresh calling to go and equip leaders using the ' stay sane through change' concept.

So my fresh message is this: Take courage that you the leader (emerging or developed; inexperienced or experienced), can use times of change as a fulcrum to propel yourself to skyrocketing success. That you could count the disruptions you encounter during periods of *external* and *internal* changes as a rudder to use in steering the boat of your organization to a rock solid position.

So what are these external and internal changes that we face as leaders?

Change in today's world

Today's rapidly changing landscape of globalization and increasing use of technology continues to create an atmosphere of violence, uncertainty, complexity and ambiguity (VUCA). Technology is redefining almost every issue in our personal, career and business lives. The way we live, eat, sleep, interact, work, move around, and relax are all being redefined. I recently read how a big financial organization has designed a work environment in which the employees have no fixed work station- a no laptop, no mobile –phone work place (2). This concept revolves around the workers sharing workstations that can be rotated at any time and is not allocated to a particular individual. Now that's a huge difference that can affect a worker to the core of their very being.

This impact of technology is huge not only on *how* we work, but also *what* we do- on the actual job functions and responsibilities of today. The World Economic Forum has depicted that we are entering the fourth Industrial revolution in which some of the jobs in existence today will not be there ten years from now (3). For instance, consider the librarian whose job function is facing redefinition because of availability of information at the click of a mouse or touch on a mobile device. Another example is the travel agent, whose job is increasingly being taken on by travel websites. These are changes that are affecting workers to the core. Their professional identities are being shaken.

Globalization, on the other hand, is creating political and socio-economic conditions that were hitherto unpredictable. We are facing the reality that the world has moved from where it was a few years back. And like it or not, we have to adapt.

Apart from these two *external* agents of change – technology and globalization-, we continue to face huge *internal* changes in our work place and organizations that also continue to call for us to adapt or be left out. The coach of a major sports team battles with losing a major player and/or loss of camaraderie amongst his team members. Such an internal change requires rebuilding trust and new team formation when a new team member is introduced.

The task of leading millennials and younger generations in a multi-generational workforce is also an internal issue many workplaces have to deal with. And the list goes on.

The complex nature of the changes is only one aspect that makes them formidable. When we consider that these changes are happening so rapidly sometimes at the speed of real time tweets, that gives us little or no room to adapt before another set of changes happen, you can begin to imagine, why this VUCA world calls for new solutions.

The huge changes are coming at unfathomable rapid speed

Not only are they big, but the changes are rapid, not giving you enough time to adjust to one before another one is introduced. For instance, the small business marketer after overcoming the learning curve finally got used to the new rules of engagement of the giant social media-Facebook. All of a sudden, Facebook algorithms changes and so do the rules.

Having considered the impact of change on our world and on you the leader at a personal level, pertinent questions are:

- How can you continue to function as a leader amidst all these complex changes?
- How can you continue to lead your organization when the rules are constantly changing?
- How can you guide your team members who have been impacted by the huge change around them?

All these are relevant questions begging for answers.

The fact is finding answers to these and similar questions call for new thinking, new levels of awareness and new combinations of leadership skill sets and styles.

Such new ways of envisioning and enacting leadership are the themes of this book.

What's in this book for you?

Stay Sane Through Change ® for Leaders will equip you as a leader on how to use the power of purpose, strengths, imagination leading to innovation and influence (PSII) to lead your team and/or organization during times of change.

I have discussed in the chapters that follow how leaders are using the following four principles to lead their teams and organizations during this complex times of change:

1. The Power of the Big Picture that encompasses Your Purpose
2. The Power of Your Strengths
3. The Power of Imagination that Spurs Innovation and
4. The Power of Community

As a leader, you can use these leadership principles while:

- Developing your personal leadership
- Leading a team in your workplace- small business or corporation
- Leading groups in the community
- Leading teams in your non-profit or charity organizations

You will glean insights from the stories that will enable your leadership while:

- Leading in times of personal changes
- Leading during transitions in your organization
- Combating *internal* and *external* change factors in your workplace and industry

Stay Sane Through Change ® for Leaders will equip you to:

- use the power of imagination to craft out-of-the-box innovative solutions to get your organization out of the loop during a crisis
- tap into the opportunities created by technology and thereby ride the waves of disruption
- tap into the power of influence provided by strategic use of social media to engage your community of followers during periods of change
- handle resistors of change through effective communications and results-oriented conversations

The leadership-themed stories in this book are of men and women who have faced various formidable and scary challenges in their personal and/or team/organizational leadership situations. These leaders come from a wide range of industries- public institutions, healthcare, academics, human resources, fashion and financial services. Though their industrial backgrounds are different, these leaders have one thing in common. They have all used the periods of changes to build on their personal leadership while cultivating resilience in their team members. You will be inspired by the stories of these leaders and will be motivated to, just like them, use periods of internal and external changes to steer your organization to a rock solid position.

As a means of quick reference, you will also find a section containing powerful questions to provoke your thoughts and guide you in the right direction while leading during times of change

So come on, ride the waves of disruption and get equipped to tap into the opportunities presented by periods of changes in your organization.

Powerful Questions for Leading Through Times of Change

These are some general visioning and implementation oriented questions to help you direct your action plans for leading successfully through periods of internal and external changes. The list is by no means exhaustive but is starting points to guide your decision-making towards successful execution strategies.

Personal Leadership

1. What are the real issues in this scenario? (This will help you separate facts from fiction, realities from fantasies and ultimately manage your emotions.)
2. What might the future look like if we successfully go through this change?
3. What's in this change for me? (This is useful for envisioning the future and is relevant for both unexpected changes that you did not create as well as intentional changes In other words- What's in this change for me?

   On the contrary,
4. What might the future look like if this change scenario is bumped/not managed well/ripples into more catastrophes i.e. the worst case scenario?

5. What will I need to successfully manage this change? Which of my strengths can be brought into play?
6. Who are my heroes/mentors- what do I know that they did when passing through this type of adversity?
7. How can the experience of leading this change bring out the best in me?
8. What kind of leadership skills might I develop or hone better if I strategically manage this change?
9. How may I bring my past leadership stories and lessons learned from them to play in this current situation of change
10. How can I connect the dots between my past leadership stories and this present change scenario?

Organizational Leadership/Team Leadership

1. What kind of organization would we become if we successfully manage this change?
2. How are other industries tapping into opportunities created by change
3. Is there an example of another industry that we can model to ride on the waves of disruption in our industry?

4. Will the approach of strategic partnering with other companies help us make more of this change situation?
5. Do we need to narrow our niche to focus more on a competitive advantage we have based on this change scenario?
6. How can we tap into the strengths of our team members to better position our company and put us in a better frame work for success?

Chapter Two

The Power of Purpose

'Purpose' has to do with the reason for the existence of an individual or entity. It identifies why you are here and what your organization exists to do – her mission. It portrays the big picture of everything that concerns you and/or your organization.

The value of recognizing and redefining one's personal purpose and the purpose of an organization during periods of change cannot be overemphasized. In fact, in order to use times of change as a pivot to steer your organization to a rock solid position, you need to take some time to redefine your purpose- the very reason for your existence.

The power of purpose in staying sane during periods of change is well illustrated in the example of the public library. It is a case in which both the individual- the librarian- and the organization – the public library- both have their purpose intertwined in a period of complex change posed by rapid advances in technology.

The following story is how the public library- a giant public institution in the national landscape of many countries all over the world redefined her purpose and that of its many professional staff members- the librarians. It demonstrates how they reinvented themselves amidst the wake of a threat of becoming irrelevant.

The Public Library redefines her purpose

Of the many industries and organizations that are seeing a vast impact on their functioning in the age of rapid globalization and technology, the library occupies a key strategic example.

This is because one of the core missions of the library lies very much on the intersection between globalization, technology and changing demographics. This mission is that of providing access to information. Traditionally this mission has been accomplished through provision and circulation of books, periodicals/magazines and multimedia (audio and video) products. This list of information resources provided through the library has rapidly advanced to include e-books and increasing number of electronic media and gadgets.

This core purpose of these age-old institutions is intertwined with the big picture of today's huge changes imposed by the rapid availability of information via a variety of other instantly available means. The internet with its continuously vast information and communities of knowledge (Wikipedia etc.) aided by huge search engines as Google have been in our society for a while. Thereafter we as a society became more comfortable with virtual reference. In more recent times, newer adoptions of social media, and crosses between media and the publishing industries such as iTunes podcasts and the like continue to increase the multiple numbers of outlets from which information can be retrieved. Thus the traditional library is at the raw end of the transformation imposed by technology

Looking at this rapid 'invasion' of their core purpose for existence, many libraries serving various facets of the population - academic, public/local-are reinventing ways of doing things in order to remain relevant to the various patrons they are serving. Many libraries are adapting to the new paradigm of not being the *sole* provider of information through innovative approaches to their structure and functioning in various facets (1). In fact, the adoption of innovative approaches by the library has in many cases been all-encompassing in the following ways:

- Adopting an innovative culture
- encouraging their staff to be innovative
- launching innovative outreaches to their communities

- tapping into technology itself to provide innovative ways of doing things such as reserving carrels
- designing innovative spaces and
- launching innovative programs

What is noteworthy is that in each of these adaptations, these libraries are keeping true to their core purpose-provision of information and access to it.

Taking 'staying relevant' to a new level

One of the key running themes in this book is how you as a leader can ride the waves of disruption in your industry and use it to steer your organization to a rock solid position.

The leaders at Arlington Heights (Illinois) Memorial Library (AHML) -- have done just that (2). They have taken the topic of 'staying relevant' to a new level through their 'marketplace in a public library' approach. This is one of the many examples of the innovative approaches different public libraries are adopting in order to stay relevant.

This innovative approach is in the design of the library space and the shelving of the books. Dewey decimal classification is an age old standard for book classification and it serves its purpose very well.

However in the marketplace in the public library approach, the leadership at AHML has taken an idea from another industry- the bookstores- and taken elements of it to use in the design of their shelving.

While keeping some of its real estate section organized in the 'traditional' library way, a special section of this library was redesigned to feature books in a bookstore-style manner. (This was done at an appropriate time when the whole library was undergoing building renovation and staffing re-organization). Instead of having the books displayed with the spine out as in regular shelves, the marketplace displays new and popular books with their covers as you find in bookstores. The book display in this market place section are still classified (not Dewey) but under the various categories e.g. non-fiction- cookbook, or fiction- mystery. However since patrons can walk around the shelves and see books displayed with the actual book covers, their interest has been piqued more.

The leaders at AHML worked with a group of selectors in rolling out this program. These selectors consulted with the Information services team of the library to find out what customers asked for the most. Based on this information, books are selected to be displayed in the marketplace section.

The good thing about how this implementation of the marketplace in the library was carried out is that other elements of library functioning were considered alongside (it was not done in isolation). The implementation was executed in a way that did not add additional burden to other parts of the library's functioning and operation. So while staying relevant to their core purpose through the marketplace, other library functions such as ordering, cataloguing and processing were considered parallel to the integration.

Essentially the purpose that the marketplace in the library serves is that of an improved form of browsing and discovery. The leaders saw it as a form of shelving and merchandising. Therefore they have appropriately used principles of merchandising – having the book's cover image face out, grouping like colours and images and pleasant display symmetry- all to attract the patron to pick the book/item and check it out

Thus, purpose is engrained in this marketplace in the library approach- making it easier for the patrons to discover the information they may require and also making it easier for them to check it out.

Using this system, the AHML has reported that circulation of books from the marketplace is 20% higher than that for their previous 'New Books and New Movies' section. Thus, in offering patrons opportunities to browse through their collection in a more visual and vivid display in a 'marketplace within the library' section, these library leaders are staying relevant to their core mission.

Continuous evaluation and feedback is key to success of change initiative

During its initial period of implementation of the marketplace in the library- a re-configuration of their structural design and one of their key offerings-, the leaders at Arlington Heights (Illinois) Memorial Library (AHML) welcomed feedback from the users the patrons.

In addition, they set up a system for continuous evaluation of the effect of the operation of the marketplace on the overall functioning of other departments of the library.

 Based on the feedback received, the leaders at AHML discovered that while shelving operations for the marketplace is easier, pulling holds for patrons who require the items for borrowing was harder. With this information, the leaders made an adjustment through a change in their pull list structure.

In addition, in considering the feedback from the patrons, the leaders have had extra signage installed in the library. This has helped the patrons find what they are looking for more easily.

Moving forward with the power of their newly redefined purpose and newly deciphered strengths

The leadership at AHJL found that the highlight of their marketplace section is having a "Trending" category where books on current trending topics are displayed. This discovery highlighted a newly deciphered strength they envisioned they could tap into. So the library design was updated so that this trending section is the first collection that patrons see when they enter the marketplace.

For instance, if there is current news of a politician signing a trade agreement with a certain nation, the librarians will put relevant items related to that news in the trending section of the marketplace. This may be a relevant book on that topic and/or a periodical such as a celebrities' magazine with a feature on that politician.

Thus the library leaders tapped into this opportunity. presented by their new strength overlaid on the purpose and big picture of their organization.

Furthermore, with increasing numbers of books becoming available to the library, the library staff members have devised means of making this marketplace in the library section work for them without negative impact on the overall functioning of the library as a whole.

Key takeaways from the public library redefine her purpose story:

The leaders at the library rode the waves of disruption by taking an example from an industry similar to theirs in the type of clientele served- people who love to read books.

They took a key idea used by bookstores who serve the same clientele of book readers- the idea of displaying books face out so that the browsers can see more about the books through the cover displays and thereby be more likely to loan them out. This ultimately leads to better access to books and increased circulation- a key purpose of the library being served

For leaders of all organizations:

- Which industries can you borrow ideas from in order to tap into opportunities presented by technology and rapid complex changes?

For leaders of public institutions and non-profit organizations:

If you are leading a non-profit that has to demonstrate its continued relevance amidst changes in your particular environment,

- Which waves of disruption can you ride to steer your organization to a rock solid position?
- Which innovative ideas can you take on to redefine your purpose?
- Which areas of your organizational structure can you infuse re-defined purpose into-
    - your staff,
    - your work place,
    - the way you are serving your members,
    - the way you are raising funds?

Chapter Three

The Power of Strengths

In the previous chapter, I demonstrated the importance of purpose-your personal leadership purpose and your organizational purpose- and its power in delineating new pathways of action during periods of internal and external changes. With the power of purpose, the giant age-old public institution- the public library- is redefining herself and staying relevant amidst turbulent changes.

The discussion in this chapter is focused on the importance of strengths- your personal leadership strengths and your organizational strengths.

Simply put, strengths define your capabilities, what you are good at, and in many cases, the parameters underlying your strength are what sets you apart from others. An organization's strengths set her apart from similar organizations in the industry and give her a competitive edge.

In order to be able to operate in an environment of *external* and *internal* changes you as a leader need to be able to redefine your strengths and employ these strengths maximally in your leadership functions. In addition, you need to have a fresh kaleidoscopic view of the strengths of your organization

During times of change, bringing your strengths to play to operate maximally requires innovative thinking and agility that enables sound decision-making at the speed of constant change. It requires the constant strategic use of your strengths so that you are always putting the right foot forwards in different change scenarios

So in staying sane as a leader in this rapid technology age, you may need to decipher your strengths once again and then re-configure how you use them to lead or manage change in order to get your organization into a rock solid position. This often calls for employing your strengths in new dimensions such as tackling resistance to change.

The following story is an example of how leaders of a change initiative drove transformation through partnering with a cadre of professionals who are at the heart of the change.

Using Your Strengths Maximally to Drive Transformation

The wide increase in health care costs in the United States has called for the design of innovative care systems that provide value to the patient while decreasing the overall cost on the health care system.

Health care administrators have in recent years asked similar questions posed to practitioners of other professions:

- How can we ride the waves of disruption created by technology and globalization to create innovative solutions that will reduce the imminent threats in our industry?

As it were, since there is a rapid shift of demographics in the United States (and in the whole world at large) due to longer longevity, a third major factor compounds the changing scenario within the health care industry. This is the issue of a rapidly changing demographics -an increase in aging population.

At the raw end of this shift in dynamics in the healthcare industry are physicians of various specialities. The following illustration is focussed on how healthcare administrators are seeking to collaborate with orthopedic surgeons to effect changes in health care environment to deliver a cost-effective value driven solution to patient care.

The pertinent question in this change initiative is:

- How can health care administrators and orthopaedic surgeons form an alliance that will work well in helping patients get the care they need (and get their tensile strength back) at a lesser cost to the health care delivery system?

Here are the key challenges faced in this huge change scenario:

The traditional physician speciality-categorized hospital-centric system of health care delivery is being revamped. Rather than having just one hospital department take care of the patient, the health care system is favouring a longer patient-driven life cycle care that calls for a network of physicians and care givers.

Traditionally, orthopaedic surgeons have been the supplier of care in a system where they got paid on a fee-for service basis (called the First Curve) (1). However, in the new system, the approach is a fee-for value (which is named the Second Curve). The second curve approach necessarily calls for serving more patients at a higher level of quality, safety and service. The ultimate result of operating on this second curve system is that it will be at a lower cost to the health care system. In addition, the second curve favors a less hospital-centric approach with the value being defined by the patient and not the provider (1).

Now consider the challenges being posed to the orthopaedic surgeon who has spent years training to become one in an environment of the previous health care system (First Curve) that favored him/her as a specialist with the bargaining power of the supplier. In the new paradigm of the second curve, much adaptation is being asked of him that may be shaking him/her to the core of his professional identity. As a professional of this cadre, he has developed autonomy that comes with the trade. With the Second Curve system, the surgeon's professional autonomy is being encroached upon, while he is being asked to reduce individualized patient care (and shift to multidisciplinary care).

On the other hand,(s)he is being asked to change from a system which has worked for him to one he is not sure of. The human motivation of aversion to loss coupled with preservation of personal security and unverbalized fear of perceived threats from an unknown organizational structure are all major agents of resistance to this change.

Leveraging each other's strengths to provide innovative solutions

In proposing new collaborative solutions some senior healthcare administrators (SHCA) have looked critically at these elements of resistance to change that may be the barriers to the execution of the change by the orthopaedic surgeons.

Charles Callaghan, a senior health care administrator and his group at the Memorial Health System, Springfield, Illinois, and his group 1, 2) are working with orthopaedic surgeons to offer innovative solutions that will drive a great quality of orthopaedic care at an affordable cost.

On their part, these senior health care administrators are offering solutions that will enable the orthopaedic surgeons to adapt to their professional repositioning better. They are approaching the surgeons with practical, objective and timely priorities that are patient-oriented.

The orthopaedic surgeons on the other hand, who work in this optimized partnership, are able to see beyond the threats of the changes. Rather they utilize this change dynamics to leverage their professional strength in association with the SHCA to bring a new value-driven product- musculoskeletal integrated care pathway to the health care marketplace.

It is hoped that this integrated care pathway will provide a framework for detailing essential steps in the care of patients across the entire episode of care. And the far-reaching result- with the use of the system, the partnership of orthopaedic surgeons and SHCA at Memorial Health System hope it will reduce hospital charges, length of stay without negative effective on patient outcomes.

Collaboration to implement change and achieve desired objectives

The key element in this paradigm of change is collaboration between different stakeholders of the change initiative. This collaboration is between highly skilled leadership professionals- healthcare administrators- and super-skilled orthopaedic surgeons. The goal of the collaboration is to provide an innovative viable care product to meet the needs of the Second Curve of health care system that is being effected in the environment of rapid technology and increasing aging population dynamics of today.

In setting the agenda for the implementation and the execution of this change initiative, the SHCA identified the importance of securing a buy-in from their would be partners- the highly skilled orthopaedic surgeons. Apart from this, they approached it from a collaborative approach with the ultimate goal that each partner in the collaboration will benefit from it. However, the SHCA did their homework well before launching out. Here are some key principles from the way these healthcare administrators drove the transformation that was necessary to tap into the opportunities created by this seemingly hard change.

The health care administrators:

- planned ahead- (this fact cannot be overemphasized)
- Identified possible elements of resistance to execution
- Looked at what happened in other industries undergoing waves of change and identified key lessons they could translate to the health care industries
- Approached their would-be partners with dignity appreciating where they were coming from
- Set a superordinate goal for the partnership – creation of a new value-driven integrated musculoskeletal substitute product which requires each

of the parties to leverage their substitute powers- the HCAs- their buying power while the orthopaedic surgeons- their supplier power

- The superordinate goal- the big agenda creates a win-win-solution for the two parties and ultimately their organization at large
- In focusing on the big agenda, small/minor agendas (personal agendas of either party) that undermine the big agenda will not be encouraged.
- Offered practical solutions to help them focus towards the same big goal- patient-driven outcomes- data, fact-based prioritization etc.
- Offered use of data, continuous monitoring to evaluate progress
- Provided continuous reinforcement to effect the change-continuous pull in the same direction

This powerful collaboration is helping the partners to steer their organization (and health care at large) to a rock solid position in these times of change

On the overall, this story also demonstrates how to handle resistors of change through effective communications and coaching style conversations

Key takeaways from the orthopaedic surgeons' story:

1. A win-win collaboration between different stakeholders of a change initiative can help tap into opportunities in a maximal way thereby strengthening their organization
2. Effective conversations and open line of communications between change leaders and implementers of change can help alleviate resistance to change and results-oriented transformation

Chapter Four

The Power of Imagination Leading to Innovation

In the earlier chapters of this book, I have illustrated how leaders are tapping into the power of purpose and the power of strengths and using them to ride on waves of disruption in their industry. In those illustrations, I mentioned how imaginative outside-the box-thinking has enabled some leaders to come up with innovative approaches of re-defining themselves when faced with the threat of becoming irrelevant.

Imagination is a powerful tool in navigating through periods of both internal and external changes. In order to be able to operate in a strong mode of imaginative thinking, you as a leader need to be agile-swift, responsive and quick-thinking

Your agility is closely linked to not being attached too much to a mode of operation or a set of status quo conditions. You as a leader need to have your antennae up to design changes in your workplace environment and respond decisively to them. In fact, an agile can anticipate changes in his industry before they happen and use that opportunity to be an agent of disruption, designing new pathways of profit in the industry before others latch onto it.

Agility and this ability to adapt quickly to new modes of operation have come into play in the adoption of rapid changes in technology by many industries today.

Adoption of technology by Human Resources entities

But this adoption is not limited to those whose core industries is itself technology such as tech giants like Microsoft (1). It is now becoming important for other organizations to adapt or be left behind and become obsolete.

The Human Resources Industries is a key example of this. In his white paper, Vijay Nachimuthu of AltaFlux a SAP enterprise software provider company has called for the human resources industry to use this adoption of the cloud technology to simplify human resources workflow and thereby boost productivity (2). He advised that in addition, the human resources industry could also use this adoption as an opportunity to extend itself from the image of being just a tactical support function

This call for change is not easy for many human resources (HR) organizations especially for those who have spent lots of money and time on installing and customizing on-premises software" to perform core HR functions such as benefits, time and attendance, and systems of record.

So the key agent of inertia is –
- How do we regain the investment that we have spent over many years on the in-house software?
- Why would we need to invest another sum of money in another solution?

But the adoption of HR cloud technology offers much more benefits and the move to invest in digital HR offers more return on investment that if properly tapped into, would be of value not just the HR but the whole organization. According to Nachimuthu. these include opportunities to use the cloud for employee engagement (which is key in a multigenerational workplace) and provision of access to crucial and instant data that drives business. He calls on HR to use these additional advantages of digital HR as a stepping stone to becoming a strategic partner at the C-suite table, helping to make forward-moving decisions for their various organizations.

The leadership of Brooks Brothers is one organization that is doing just that.

'Tailoring' a new HR suite for a fashion juggernaut

As a juggernaut of the fashion industry Brooks Brothers has been in operation for many years (since 1818 to be exact). Since that time to date, they have become 'an institution that has shaped the American style of dress through fashion innovation, fine quality, personal service, and exceptional value in our products' (3). With over 265 stores in the United States and Canada and more than 250 in international locations, the organization is indeed a global enterprise. Alongside this huge success is the need to provide a fulfilling work environment for its employees. As far as the leadership of this company knew, they had been effective in hiring and onboarding new talents and performing other 'traditional' HR functions. However, with the HR industry experiencing tremendous changes impacted by the wide adoption of technology in unforeseen areas, the leadership at Brookes Brothers have had to rethink their process of talent management.

Their old cut-to-fit model of HR also required some innovation to match their promises. This old system was a legacy on-premises paper based payroll system that had been retrofitted to perform many HR duties. In the past few years, Brookes Brothers started using

SAP's SuccessFactors, (by IBM Global Business Services) cloud software for its HR functions (4).

Moving from 'the dark ages to the cloud' -talent management in a new era

As Justin Watras, director of talent management and organizational effectiveness for Brooks Brother said the adoption of cloud technology was like moving from the 'dark ages to the cloud'.

However, the process of change was not without any hitches. In order to get buy-in from senior management of his organization, Watras had to employ his imaginative thinking.
The question is:

- What else could this cloud technology do for us?
- How can we validate its value with management?

In communicating the change to the managers of the company, Watras approached it by allowing them see that it is not just going to be a change to yet another system but a change that will put them in ownership and control. He made them to see the advantages of the cloud, one of which is having instant access to their employee data -compensation, performance, biographical - that puts them in a position to empower and grow their people.

The results of imaginative thinking

Adoption of cloud technology by this organization has resulted in an elimination of 15 paper-based processes, 50% (5) increase in employee data efficiency and a 10% increase in productivity due to the decreased amount of administration time spent on talent hiring and onboarding (4).

In addition, people analytics such as employee turnover and compensation are now available via the cloud platform. This enables HR to present more meaningful data that correlate with business outcomes to the executive management team.

Watras sees more prospects for this cloud adoption by his organization as 'repositioning HR within the organization so that it's no longer viewed as a cost sink but rather a value contributor'.

Thus, adopting this change and tapping into the opportunities presented by it provides a forum for Brook Brothers HR leaders to steer their organization into a rock solid position

Which issues of leading during periods of change do you currently face?

How can you use imaginative thinking to craft out possible solutions to the particular change?

Key takeaways from the Brookes Brothers adopting technology for HR

- A leader needs to be agile in order to perceive changes in the environment of his industry and thereby design new pathways to tap into opportunities presented by those changes.

- The power of imagination leading to innovation is not limited to crafting new solutions, but can be used in various facets of leading changes such as communicating to stakeholders and securing a buy-in to the change initiative

Chapter Five

The Power of Influence Through Community

In the previous chapters of this book, I have discussed how you a leader can tap into the power of your leadership/organizational purpose, strengths and imagination to steer your organization to a rock solid position amidst the complex changes in our world today. The stories in those chapters demonstrate that the use of a combination of purpose, strength and imagination can create new pathways of action to propel you and your organization into a firm position despite the turbulence of change.

In particular, the previous chapter emphasized the need for you, a leader to be agile, and have your antennae up to detect signals in your external environment and understand the trends of imminent disruption in your industry. This is so that you can open up yourself to the power of imaginative thinking, to decipher which of your strengths to put into play so as to reinforce your purpose and the big picture of your organization.

This present chapter illustrates the power of influence in leading through times of change. Influence is indeed a powerful leadership tool and periods of change call for the ability to use this powerful tool maximally to your advantage. The following story illustrates how an organization used technology to magnify the power of influence and use it to their advantage at a critical period of organizational rebranding.

Embracing technology and using it to buoy effect of change on your community

In the last few years, the big financial services firm ING US shifted their emphasis from general financial services to that of retirement planning and re-branded to become Voya Financial (1).

In taking on this huge rebranding, this company tapped into the power of influence via community using the great influencer in our technology enhanced world- social media.

With this rebranding, every stakeholder of the company is greatly impacted- the loyal customers, would-be clients, employees, investors, the board of directors and senior management.

Here is how ING U.S rebranded to 'Voya Financial' and bought into play the tools of the social media giant LinkedIn to raise awareness for this rebranding process. It is a good example of how technology can be used to buoy the effects of change on an organization's followers, team members and community

As Ann Glover, the Chief Marketing Officer of Voya Financial stated: 'the spreading of the news about our rebranding, LinkedIn was a very important piece of a complicated puzzle" (2).

Yes, rebranding is a huge change that has many pieces forming part of a big puzzle. The leaders had to ask many critical questions during the whole process. One key question is:

How can my organization 'translate' the long history of credibility to that of a new brand?

As the theme of this book conveys it, navigating through changes in your organization -either internal or environmental- can pose many challenges. Thus, in Voya's case, a major one such as shifting the core service offerings could indeed be overwhelming. The leadership had to think it through strategically and plan ahead as the change y hinges on the core of the organization's identity.

A huge complimentary challenge that comes with such a gigantic change is"

-   How can we do this without an adverse effect on our profits?

Put it in a more proactive way the question is,

-   How can my organization use this period of rebranding to reposition herself for even more success than it had before the rebranding?

In using LinkedIn as an influencer tool to help communicate and engage its audience, Voya Financial tapped into the power of community to drive this change without too much confusion and in a manner that positioned them for profitability afterward.

Continuous Communication at multiple touch points

When Voya Financial embarked on their LinkedIn campaign, they identified all stakeholder segments that would be affected by the change:

- employees,
- customers,
- financial advisors

The act of bringing together seventy-three legal entities to become one was, to say the least intimidating.

So with multiple segments to address and a need for clarity in what the new brand offers to communicate, Voya Financial could not afford to use a one or few-point "touch and go' solution. Rather Voya Financial leveraged a robust solution of continuous multiple touch points to engage all the various target audiences on LinkedIn.

Amongst other things, tapping into two of LinkedIn Marketing Solutions- Sponsored Content and Display

Ads, combined with LinkedIn's tight targeting tools, Voya Financial was able to reach its target demographics of its old and would –be –clients- affluent professionals and financial advisors.

Using your employees as mini-change agents to communicate change

Voya Financial also tapped into the power of influence provided by their large number of employees (almost five thousand) who are already present on LinkedIn. With the help of the Voya marketing team, employees of the company also became min-communicators of the change through the act of making changes to their LinkedIn profiles.

In addition, through LinkedIn's tool of Company Page combined with LinkedIn advertising strategy, Voya Financial was able to able to build more awareness to the new company brand.

As these LinkedIn company pages are followed by both their employees and the company's target audiences, these 'followers' also become mini-agents who could share Voya's stories through sharing the company pages' updates.

Thus, all these chains of reactions created by the Voya Financial's LinkedIn community become a powerful influence to translate the long existing credibility of ING, US to that of their new brand-Voya Financial. This, in turn, positioned the company for procuring more business and remaining profitable after the huge rebranding

Using a multipoint strategy, Voya Financial tapped into the power of influence provided through the strategic use of social media to their advantage to drive their organization into a rock solid position of a powerful retirement planning organization.

So the question now is:

- What are the disruptions in your own industry as a leader?
- How can you ride the waves of these disruptions to steer your organization to a rock solid position?
- How can you tap into the opportunities provided by strategic use of social media as a great influencer to your advantage?

Key takeaways from the Voya Financial story:

- As a leader in this technology-driven world, you can strategically tap into the power of influence presented by social media and use it to drive transformation, effect rebranding and re-position your organization for growth at various phases.

- Empowering your employees and team members to become change leaders who drive transformation will help you get a better results-oriented outcome on your change initiatives.

Chapter Six

Moving Forward with the Combined Power of PSII

In the preceding chapters of this book I have elucidated how you can use the following to your advantage during times of change:

1.   The Power of the Big Picture that encompasses Your Purpose

2.   The Power of Your Strengths

3.   The Power of Imagination that Spurs Innovation and

4.   The Power of Influence through Community

I have illustrated how you as a leader can use these four elements to steer your organization into rock solid position during periods of change. I have used stories of leaders from various industries- a public institution, healthcare, fashion industry/human resources entity and financial services to draw out key principles you can use to stay sane through the changes occurring in our complex world of today. In fact, these facts are relevant today more than ever before.

So even if you do not have a chaotic external change being posed on you, the fact of the rapid change being created by technology and globalization poses an environment of change in which you have to operate in. Invariably you have some changes being 'forced on you by the very nature of today's world.

In addition to these huge overall change experienced by every organization, your particular industry or corporate body may be facing some unique changes. There are disruptions in every industry due to rapid advances in technology and globalization

Consider the book publishing industry for an example and let's take one aspect of it- creating book covers. When I wrote my first book the first *Stay Sane Through Change*, my co-author and I used the services of a 'vantage/vanity' self-publisher. We were given just one version of a front cover image. We were quite grateful that the version was in sync with our message; otherwise, that would have been another issue to navigate around.

By the time I wrote my second book, *Strength to Deliver*, things were quite different. There were many more options to get beautiful professional cover images at reasonable prices. When I republished this second book via a new publishing company of my own, I decided to use a crowdsourced platform to get the cover image. To my amazement, within a very short time, I literally had up to thirty different versions created by freelancers who bided for the project. When I had my final cover image from the chosen 'finalist' in the bidding, it was very much to my liking because we had virtually co-created it. In addition, during the process of selection of the finalists for the project, I had seen lots of other versions that boosted my creativity on the subject of the book. If I decided to write book derivatives based on the original subject, I had up to four different pre-finalist cover images I could go back to.

In more recent times, I have had covers made for my books and information products even at a faster rate and have a choice of such crowdsourced platforms to use depending on the type of pricing I aim for. I have seen other authors send their crowdsourced covers to their social media followers to help them choose which is best.

Now, this is just one aspect of book writing and publishing that has seen rapid changes over the course of the last few years. There are many more innovative ways that have evolved in the industry.

So the age of disruptive changes have come upon us and the effect will continually be magnified over time.

So take on the principles discussed in Stay Sane Through Change® for Leaders.

Use the section on 'powerful questions for leading through times of change' to direct your decision making.

Grab the insights from the various examples of leaders illustrated in this book and modify them through imaginative thinking to suit your own change scenario.

Go on, ride the waves of disruption and tap into opportunities presented by change with the combined powers of your purpose, strength, imagination leading to innovation and influence through community.

Go on and steer your organization to a rock solid position.

NOTES

Chapter One

(1). Webster, F. David, and Adeleye, Tolulope, A., *Stay Sane Through Change: How to Rise Above the Challenges of Life's Complex Transitions* (Martinsburg, WV: Holy Fire Publishing, 2005)

(2). Chad Bray, No Laptop, No Phone, No Desk: UBS Reinvents the Work Space November 3, 2016 https://mobile.nytimes.com/2016/11/04/business/dealbook/ubs-bank-virtual-desktops-london.html? Accessed December 4, 2016

(3). Global Challenge Insight: Employment, Skills and the Workforce Strategy for the Fourth Industrial Revolution Report http://www3.weforum.org/docs/WEF_Future_of_Jobs.pdf World Economic Forum – (January 2016)

Chapter Two

(1). Anthony Molaro and Leah H. White (Eds.) The Library Innovation Toolkit: Ideas, Strategies and Programs. ALA, Chicago, 2015

(2). Daisy Porter Reynolds. *Like A Kid in a Candy Store- Marketplaces in Public Libraries,* p.125. In Anthony

Molaro and Leah H. White (Eds.) The Library
Innovation Toolkit: Ideas, Strategies and Programs.
ALA, Chicago, 2015

Chapter Three

(1). Callahan,Charles, Adair, Daniel; Bozic, Kevin J.,
Manning, Blaine T., Saleh, Jamal K and Saleh, Khaled
J., *Orthopaedic Surgery Under National Health Reform: An
Analysis of Power, Process, Adaptation, and Leadership: AOA
Critical Issues. The Orthopaedic Forum,* Journal of Bone &
Joint Surgery - American Volume. 96(13):e111-1-6, July
2014.

(2). Manning, Blaine , Callahan, Charles D., Brooke S.
Robinson, Adair, Daniel and Saleh, Khaled J. *Overcoming
Resistance to Implementation of Integrated Care Pathways in
Orthopaedics,* The Journal of Bone and Joint Surgery
95(14):e1001-6 · July 2013□

Chapter Four

(1). Mary Jo Foley. *Microsoft continues its transition from the
Windows company to a cloud company* October 20, 2016
http://www.zdnet.com/article/microsoft-continues-
its-transition-from-the-windows-company-to-a-cloud-
company Accessed November 13, 2016

(2). Vijay Nachimuthu, *HR's new role as a business partner - A Seat at the C-Suite Table-* -AltaFlux whitepaper

http://www.cioreview.com/news_new/whitepaper_file/us6aAltaFlux_WhitePaper_HR_New_Role.pdf

Accessed December 4, 2016

(3). http://www.brooksbrothers.com/on/demandware.store/Sites-brooksbrothers-Site/default/AboutUs-Show

Accessed December 17, 2016

(4). Katherine Noyes. *How the cloud is transforming HR.* March 20, 2016 IDG News Service

http://www.computerworld.com/article/3049420/cloud-computing/how-the-cloud-is-transforming-hr.html

Accessed December 4, 2016

(5). Brooks Brothers refashions human resources with SuccessFactors and IBM, sees 50 percent productivity gain

https://www.successfactors.com/content/dam/successfactors/en_us/resources/case-studies/brooks-brothers-cs.pdf

Accessed December 11, 2016

Chapter Five

(1). https://corporate.voya.com/newsroom/news-releases/ing-us-inc-officially-becomes-voya-financial-inc

Accessed December 4, 2016

(2). LinkedIn Marketing Solutions- Voya Financial Case Study

https://business.linkedin.com/content/dam/me/business/en-us/marketing-solutions/case-studies/pdfs/05102016_LinkedIn_VoyaFinancialCaseStudy_MM.pdf

Accessed December 4, 2016